DOLLY Dives Deep!

By Andrew Jordan Nance
Illustrated by Anaís Balbás

Edited by Deborah Sosin
Book design and illustrations by Anaís Balbás

ISBN 979-8-218-31472-9

For anyone who was afraid to take
a risk and did it anyway.

Dolly was born in the shallow waters of a beautiful bay.

Twisting in circles, her mother labored hard
to bring her into the world.

Dolly's grandma and aunt lifted her up
for her first breath of air.

In the beginning, Dolly stayed close to her mother and the rest of the dolphin pod.

Dolly learned how to use her speed to keep safe,
her sonar to look for danger, and her beak to look for food.

She loved to play with the other little dolphins in the pod, while keeping an eye out for her mother.

One day, Dolly heard the entire pod would soon leave the safety of the bay. Was she ready?

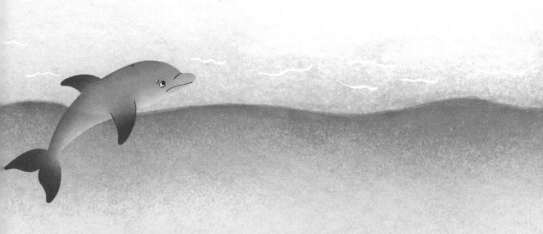

What if the waves are too high? she thought.
What if I am not strong enough?

Gathering her courage, she swam alone to the edge of the bay.
Wow, the water looks dark and deep!

I can't even see the bottom! What if I need a rest?
Dolly's heart beat faster!

She sped back to where Grandma hovered nearby.

"I'm scared," Dolly whispered.
"Speak up, dear. I can't hear so well."

"I'm scared to go into deep water!" Dolly squealed.

Grandma nudged Dolly. "Fear is a natural emotion.
It's our body's way of telling us that we need to be careful."

"Where in *your* body do you sense fear?"
Dolly paused...

"In my chest, fins, and tail."

"Excellent!" Grandma said.
"Now swim to the surface and take a deep breath."

"How did that feel?" Grandma asked, hugging Dolly.
"I'm much calmer and more focused!"

"Great! Shall we try diving even deeper?"

In the darkening ocean, Grandma swam on as Dolly struggled to keep up.

Dolly felt safer close to Grandma.
She looked around- the water
now seemed beautiful!

"What do you see?" Grandma gently asked.
"Lots of colorful fish," Dolly chirped.

"Remember how to use your sonar, Dolly?" Grandma asked.
"What do you sense outside the bay?"
Dolly focused, sending her sonar waves into the darkness.

She sensed a whale, a sunken ship, and a shark!
"Uh oh!" cried Dolly.

Grandma guided Dolly quickly to the surface for a calming breath.
"Yes, my dear, there are dangers in our world, but wonders too!"

"Will I have to face them alone, Grandma?" clicked Dolly.
"No. The dolphin pod will be there to guide you."

"But you must practice." Grandma urged.
"Remember to use your breath to stay focused
and calm if you sense danger."

When Dolly was ready, they swam back
to her mother and the others.
The calves were chasing some cod.

Each day, Dolly grew braver, taking deep breaths when she needed to focus or when she felt afraid.

When the calves were old enough to leave the bay,
the entire pod gathered together.

With loud whistles and a slap of her tail,
Grandma signaled for the dolphins to depart.

Dolly glided over to her young friends,
finally ready to dive deep into the unknown waters ahead.

Printed in the USA
CPSIA information can be obtained
at www.ICGtesting.com
LVHW062020020224
770738LV00006B/66